Lanzarote

Land of volcanoes

If the heavens suddenly seem black and the land reflects a luminous light silvery grey when walking on Lanzarote, it does not take much to imagine we are on the moon. The difference is that despite the arid lunar landscape, the volcanoes, the craters and the huge extense of lava give this island a gamut of colours. Browns, reds, ochres, golds, greys and blacks contrast with the green of the crop fields, the vines and the palm trees, with the clean, sparkling white of its houses and villages and, especially, with the blue and emerald of the transparent waters of the Atlantic Ocean.

Most of the more than 100 volcanoes that there are on this island, declared a Biosphere Reserve by UNESCO in 1993, are in Timanfaya National Park and are the result of the eruptions which took place in the 18th century in central and eastern Lanzarote. Others are almost 4,000 years old, like the volcano of La Corona, which caused a huge "*malpaís*" ("badlands" ie land covered with solidified lava) in the North East and South East of the island.

Lanzarote is 1,000 kilometres from the Iberian Peninsula and less than 150 from the

Malpaís

Famara

coast of Africa. It is the most northerly of the Canary Islands and the 4th largest with a surface area of 795 square kilometres. Its 213 kilometre coastline is made up of huge cliff formations, such as Famara, numerous sandy beaches, small coves and flooded volcanic tubes that form the famous "*jameos*".

History and Nature

Lanzarote was the first of the Canary Islands to be reached and settled by European navigators in their attempt to colonise the archipelago. It was from here that they set out to conquer the other islands. The primitive Guanche inhabitants called Lanzarote an island that had been inhabited since Neolithic times, *Titeroy-*

Gatra. The origin of the Guanches are not quite clear though it is   probable that they came to the Canary Islands from North Africa in the 1st and 2nd centuries A.D.

The Romans called Lanzarote *Purpuraria* owing to the abundance of "orchilla", a lichen from which they extracted dyes. Genovese merchants, Mallorcans, Catalans, Castilians and the Portuguese began to make voyages to the Canary Islands as of the end of the 13th century. Thus, between 1320 and 1339, the Italian navigator, Lancelotto Malocello´s vessel reached the coast of Lanzarote, to which he gave his name. Later came other explorers. De Tegghia (1341), Ruis de Avendaño (1377), Peraza (1399) and contact was established with the peaceul Guanches. They were shepherds and fishermen and grew barley and wheat which they later roasted and ground to make flour for "gofio".

In the 15th century, a French Baron, Jean de Bethencourt left his palace in Normandy for the Canary Islands. In 1402, Bethencourt subdued the chief or "*mencey*" Guardafrá and conquered Lanzarote. To maintain his right of occupation, he sought the protection of King Enrique III of Castile in return for paying tribute and the island became the first in the Archipelago to be annexed to the crown of Castile as a dominion.

In the 16th and 17th centuries, Lanzarote was repopulated by Castilians , Andalucians and others from the Peninsula that make up the bulk of the present population. A few words and many place-names are all that remain of the Guanche civilization, which was almost wiped out after Bethencourt conquest. The aborigines lived in villages of open-air constructions as can be seen today in the settlement of Zonzamas, where excavations have revealed a great deal of information regarding their culture.

Due to its particular geological configuration, nature on Lanzarote is spectacular. The plants and animals have adapted to these special conditions. Apart from the lichens that coat the lava flows, the plant symbol of the island is the sweet tabaiba of a bush that can be even more than 2 metres high. However, the only group of trees worth mentioning is the palm grove at Haría. Lanzarote is an obligatory stopping-off point for a great variety of migrating birds and its waters are home to an extraordinarily rich marine fauna.

Lichens

Haría palm grove

Tourism, the main economic activity

Up until recently, agriculture (and to a lesser extent, fishing) was the predominant economic activity in most of the municipalities of Lanzarote. However, nowadays, tourism is the main source of income. Fabulous landscapes, unusual and startling, a mild climate between 18 and 24°C throughtout the year, magnificent golden beaches and plenty of leisure opportunities seem motive enough to come to the island. But there is something else, something unique that makes having chosen Lanzarote as your holiday destination a different kind of experience: the care with which not only the monuments and old buildings have been pre-served but also the appearance of a modern arquitecture that integrates into a landscape that remains untouched until this day.

Nothing is out of place on this island. There are even no advertising hoardings by the roadside and neither do the shops announce themselves with enormous letters and neon-lights. There are no electricity wires in sight, nor huge buildings . It is something that is surprising from the first moment. This preoccupation of the people of Lanzarote to preserve the environment, the traditional architecture and to keep tourism in check is owed by and large to the intuition and artistic talent of César Manrique. Born in Arrecife in 1920, Manrique was a multi-faceted: painter, sculptor, architect, ecologist, conserver of artistic heritage, urban designer and land-

Shelling of corn

The Mojón's lovers

scape artist designer. His first inspiration was the volcanic texture of Lanzarote. He was able to convince his fellow islanders that it was possible to live on tourism without making the same mistakes made elsewhere (in the country and the world). Nature is the jewel in Lanzarote´s crown, he said. His creative works can be found all over the island.

Crafts, Cuisine and Tradition

Lanzarote is a land of fine craftsmen who painstakingly produce earthen ware, ceramics and clay objects using the old basic techniques of their forebears. Also crafted are their famous string-instruments, a fundamental part of their culture, such as the timple 'lanzaroteño', its peculiar sound accompanying and enhancing the folklore of the Canaries. Likewise, Lanzarote´s weavers skilfully elaborate embroidery, rosettes, lace, baskets and hats. These and other local products can be seen and acquired at the popular street markets such as the one held every Sunday in Teguise. They can also be found during 'fiestas' and on dates announced in any village on Lanzarote.

All kinds of vegetables, the natural ingredients used in the making of traditional stews are grown in the island´s fields. The sea provides fish such "vieja", "sama" and "cherne". As on the rest of the Canary Islands, the delicious stews are seasoned with either red (paprika) or green (coriander) "mojos", and eaten with "papas arrugadas" (small potatoes cooked in their skins in very salty water). Canarios also serve with their meals 'gofio', toasted corn or wheat flour of Guanche origin.

Due to the fact that Lanzarote has mainly grown creals, the almost emblematic island dish is 'potaje de millo rolado', a maiz stew, flavoured with salt pork Neither must we forget the delicious fish 'sancocho' To drink, there is the famous 'Malvasía' wine, nowadays of *denomi-*

Selecting onions for seeding

nación de origen' (appellation d´origine) specifying Lanzarote.

The most popular traditional games and sports on the island are 'la bola' and Canary style wrestling, although there are some variations such us 'pelotamano', 'barquillos de vela latina', 'juego del palo', ´salto del pastor', ´la billarda', ´la piña', 'jotaleros' and other trials of strength competitions, either with rocks or barrels, and animal competitions

Malvasia wines (Malmsey)

A pumpkin field

Milking a goat

such as horse racing held during the 'fiestas' of the different villages.

There are many surprises to impress the visitor to Lanzarote: seas of petrified lava; columns of steam rising from a still very hot earth, enigmatic craters with multi-coloured walls, mysterious lagoons, vines among the ashes, each protecting the other from the wind, wild beaches with transparent water. All in all, a really unusual paradise to discover and fall in love with.

Gofio (roasted corn)

Arrecife

Arrecife has been the capital of Lanzarote since 1852, when the thrust of the city, especially its fishing port, overcame the dominance of the historical and señorial town of San Miguel de Teguise, which had been devastated by an attack by Barbary pirates. Founded in the 15th century, it has a coastline bordered by the reefs from which it got its name and deep water, which makes it an exceptional natural haven for fishing. There ,abundant octopus and squid, lobsters, porgys and groupers grow large as do limpets and other coastal shellfish.

In reality, it is the smallest municipality on the island although it is home to almost half the Lanzaroteño population. Its history

Municipal Park

Maritime avenue, Las Bolas bridge and the church of San Ginés

El Reducto maritime park and the Cabildo of Lanzarote

José Ramírez Cerdá Park

José Ramírez Cerdá Park

El Mercadillo Commercial Centre (Real street)

has always been inextricably linked to the sea and its two natural ports, Los Caballos and Naos. Before the constuction of the Los Marmoles dock, great care had to be taken in navigating its channels to avoid the sharp rocks lying below the surface.

Even nowadays, Arrecife still retains the character and style of a colonial fishing village. This can be seen in what is known as **Charco de San Ginés**, the original hub of the town where they built the first hermitage and several humble fishermen's cottages. It is a natural lagoon, whose quiet waters rise and fall with the tide, joined to the ocean by a small channel. This provides moorings and shelter for the little fishing boats and a modern avenue runs alongside.It is close to the lagoon where the first buildings of the town began to spring up. From there it is possible to see the islets and

Charco de San Ginés

Charco de San Ginés

Agustín de la Hoz Culture House

El Reducto maritime park

reefs which are so characteristic of the land-scape but which are mostly covered at high tide. The most important of these islets is San Gabriel or del Castillo on which Arrecife dock stands. Other islets of note are the large and lofty Islote del Frances and the Islote de los Ingleses.

The capital of Lanzarote has a calm and peaceful atmosphere despite having been turned into an important commercial centre thanks to its economic development and demographic growth. Its inhabitants throng the streets and stroll along the sea shore, the municipal park and Avenida Marítima where

Cabildo of Lanzarote

Charco de San Ginés

El Reducto Beach

León street and Castle (Real street)

the old Calle Real, now León y Castillo starts. This is the most important street in the town where the majority of the shops, restaurants and cafeterias can be found. With regards to gastronomy, Lanzaroteños prefer sea-food whether fresh or *jareado*(salted and air-dried) such as the *sanconcho canario*, boiled "vieja", or limpets with rice. The clean, fine golden sands of **Playa del Reducto** and the islote de Fermina, which is opposite, can also be found within the city boundaries.

Church of San Ginés

Iglesia de San Ginés
(San Ginés Church)

The church of San Ginés, the patron saint of Arrecife, was the first to be built in the city. Now restored, it contains the offerings and promises in the form of maps, candles and reliquaries, of the seamen and fishermen who had asked the saint for protection when in peril during storms on the high sea. In the month of August, the city commemorates the festival of San Ginés. Considered to be a great tourist attraction, for ten days there are processions, folklore festivals, wrestling competitions and fairs all over Arrecife city centre. At home, the families prepare a *"puchero de lapas"* (limpet stew) with rice, which on these occasions they call *"sopa borracha"* (drunkard's soup) in order to minimise the effects of the excesses of the "fiesta".

Large crowds also celebrate **carnival** in Arrecife enlivened by the parade of La Parranda Marinera de los Buches, which runs through the streets singing and dancing and beating the locals with their *buches* (inflated fish stomachs) to encourage them to join in the fun.

Carnival in Arrecife

Castillo de San Gabriel
(San Gabriel Castle)

The magnificent **Puente de las Bolas** bridge with its sphere-topped pillars, built over the Islote de Quemado, joins the city and San Gabriel castle. King Felipe II ordered its construction in 1574 to defend Arrecife from the frequent attacks of Barbary pirates.

Las Bolas bridge

Castle of San Gabriel and Arrecife

The castle seen from the beach

Inside of the Archaeological Museum

San José Castle

However, the castle was razed to the ground twelve years later by pirates led by the corsair Morato Arraez. Legend has it that after a heroic resistance in which men and women distinguished themselves equally, the defenders preferred to take their own lives rather than fall into the hands of the attackers to become concubines or slaves in far off lands. In 1596, the Italian architect, Leonardo Torriani rebuilt the castle in its present rectangular shape and now it houses the island´s Archeological Museum, which has exhibits from pre-hispanic times.

Inside of the castle

Castillo de San José (San José Castle)

Situated in the bay of the port of Arrecife, San José Castle was built in 1779 by order of King Carlos III to strengthen and consolidate

The castle: snack-bar

A night view of the Castle of San José

the city´s defence but specifically to relieve the hunger the threatened the Lanzaroteños, who had been left with no resources and no work. Several consecutive years of drought meant not having crops to harvest in the fields, a situation made more difficult still by the violent volcanic eruptions that brought ruin to the island and devastated the fertile soil. With the construction of the castle, popularly known as the *Fortaleza del Hambre* (Fort Hunger), the Spanish crown tried to create jobs and aid survival.

Until 1890, the castle was used as a magazine but it later fell into disuse. After restoration work carried out under the supervision of the artist César Manrique, the building has, since 1976, housed the *Museo de Arte Contemporáneo* and exhibits works of modern art by the likes of Picasso, Miró, Tapies and Manrique himself along with many other painters and sculptors both national and international.

Museum of Contemporary Art

Costa Teguise

A few miles to the north of Arrecife is Costa Teguise , one of the most important concentrations of tourist facilities on Lanzarote. It is situated for the most part within the municipality of San Miguel de Teguise. Next to golden sand coves such as Playa del Ancla, separated from each other by arms of black lava and wide open spaces are hotels, apartments, bungalows and chalets. All these buildings are inspired by the island architecture and in harmony with the volcanic environment as are the shops, restaurants and bars that provide a lively night-life.

A night view of Costa Teguise

The complex has all kinds of sports facilities available and even an **18-hole grass golf** course by which families can

Las Cucharas Beach

Costa Teguise: golf links

Bastián Beach

enjoy an Aquatic Park with swimming pools and slides. Windsurfing fans find this part of the coast the perfect place for

Aquatic Park

their favourite sport thanks to the winds which are always blowing. Las Cucharas beach is the best and most important beach on the Costa Teguise and ideal for letting yourself be carried by a sail and a board. Even if you have never been windsurfing before, there is a school close by where you can learn the sport. The warm clear water, rich with marine fauna attracts fishing enthusiasts. Nearby, are the beaches of "Los Charcos" and "Playa Bastián". This comfortable tourist resort has visitors enjoying a good holiday in its coves and on its beaches all year round thanks to the warm climate of Lanzarote.

El Ancla Beach

Los Charcos Beach

Las Cucharas Beach

Las Cucharas Beach

Sculptures at Las Cucharas Beach

El Tablillo Beach

Las Cucharas Beach

Las Cucharas Beach

Fundación César Manrique

Six kilometres to the north of Arrecife is the little village of Tahíche lying on a desert plain at the foot of a hill. This quiet village is known especially because it was there that the great Lanzaroteño artist, César Manrique, built his house. He lived in it until 1987 and later left it to his fellow citizens as a foundation. Manrique moved to Madrid in 1945 to study painting at the Escuela de Bellas Artes de San Fernando. By the end of the 1950´s he was already internationally known for his abstract works.Between 1966 and 1968 he lived in New York where his paintings were exhibited in galleries alongside those of famous painters such as Joan Miró and Max Beckmann. Nevertheless, Manrique used to say that having been born in Lanzarote would sensitise anybody and he decided to return to settle permanently on the island, which he referred to as "this burnt geology of ashes in the middle of the Atlantic". Manrique's idea was to conserve the environment, the harmony with nature and the continuation of natual processes.

César Manrique Foundation

Wind sculpture

Exhibition room

With his childhood friend and the then President of the Cabildo Insular de Lanzarote (an organisation with representatives from all the towns on the island), José Ramírez Cerdá, he managed to impose a style on the island as much in architectural terms as in physical terms. Manrique began his works without drawing up plans and developed his projects on the ground. The artist designed his house in Taro de Tahíche over five volcanic bubbles, each a different colour on a lava flow. His amazing two-storey structure added to the water spouts, the swimming pool, the palm trees and the cacti of the garden, managed perfectly to transmit this idea of making architecture fit in with a natural landscape.

The César Manrique Foundation was inaugerated in 1992, a few years before the death of its inspiration. It seeks to conserve, study and disseminate his work: paintings, drawings and sketches, the sculptures and ceramics, the photographs, the plans of pro-

Swimming-pool of the house

César Manrique

jects completed and those not. There are travelling exhibitions here and conferences of intellectuals and artists of international repute. Manrique himself considered the Foundation to be a reward for all the work done throughout his life and as a "personal legacy" bequeathed to the people of Lanzarote: "I hope that it serves to keep alive the fostering of art, the integration of architecture into nature and the environment, and to preserve the cultural and natural values of our island".

Inside views of the Foundation

Outside and gardens of the Foundation

Gardens of the Foundation

Teguise

Capital of Lanzarote from the middle of the 15th century, the historic noble town and señorial, San Miguel de Teguise was one of the first civil urban settlements in the Canaries. The town has been declared "conjunto arquitectonico historico-artistico" and lived its moment of maximum splendour in the 16th century, when most of the group of monumental buildings of what is now the old quarter was built. In these narrow, cobbled streets there are exceptional buildings: Franciscan and Dominican convents, beautiful churches, the palaces of the nobles

A view of Teguise from the Castle of Santa Bárbara

Spínola Square

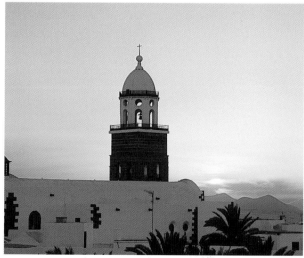

Church at dusk

Peasants

Church of Nuestra Señora de Guadalupe

Convent of San Francisco

and spacious family houses made of brick and stone with white-washed walls, large windows and comfortable carved balconies.

The city arose on the site of a *Majo* (aboriginal Lanzaroteños) hamlet, the settlement of Acatife where Teguise lived. She was the daughter of Guardafrá, the last of the island´s Guanche chiefs and the wife of Jean de Bethencourt, who conquered Lanzarote for the crown of Castile. It was princess Teguise who made peace and understanding between the followers of her father and those of her husband

Typical patio

Spínola Museum: the dining-room

possible. San Miguel de Teguise was the spiritual and administrative centre of the island, from where the expeditions left to conquer the rest of the archipelago. It was also the seat of the Marquis of Lanzarote, an institution created by Agustín de Herrera. The rapid growth of the city and its economic importance aroused the greed of the pirates and it suffered repeated attacks between the 16th and the 18th centuries during which monumental buildings and archives were destroyed. The Callejón de la Sangre (Blood Alley) recalls one of the massacres perpetrated by the pirates on the populace of the historic town.

One of the principal monuments in Teguise is the **Spinola Palace**, built in the 18th century replete with halls, a patio with a cistern,

Spínola Museum: the patio

Windmill

Street market

Palace of the Marquis

Street market

a garden and a chapel. Also worthy of note in the old quarter are señorial mansions such as the Palacio del Marqués, the **Casa de los Herrera** and the **Casa Torres**.

Notable religious buildings include the Franciscan convent of Miraflores, where a beautiful Genovese carving of Saint Francis of Assisi is kept. The convent of Santo Domingo features an original coffered ceiling.In the midst of these buildings is the **Iglesia de Nuestra Señora de Guadalupe** built in gothic style in the 15th century. However, fire and pirates both destroyed it on various occasions.

Teguise offers its visitors ample shopping opportunities in its craftshops and bazaars and the popular street market held every Sunday in its streets and squares whose stalls sell crafts made following long held traditions.Neither should it be forgotten that many of the great masters of timple making have come from Lanzarote and especially Teguise. The timple is that small traditional musical instrument that looks something like the ukelele, whose sound box is made of curved wood, giving it its characteristic jaunty sound.

Museum of the Emigrant (Santa Bárbara Castle)

Castillo de Santa Bárbara (Santa Bárbara Castle)

Away from the urban centre of Teguise, on the summit of the Guanapay volcano the Castillo de Santa Barbara, the oldest in the Canary Islands, is to be found. At first, the Genovese navigator Lancelotto Malocello built a fortification next to the extinguished crater in 1312. The history of this construction is marked by the successive raids of pirates and corsairs in 1551 ,the french pirate, "El Clérigo" and the Turk, "Cachidiablo"; in 1569 "Calafat" and in 1571, Barbary pirates under the command of Dogali "El Turquillo" lay siege to Teguise and its fortress. In 1586, the pillage by Morato Arráez compelled more than 1000 people to seek refuge in the castle. In the light of the destruction wreaked by these raids King FelipeII sent the engineer, Leonardo Torriani, who rebuilt it in 1596, with the present day rhomboid shape, watch-towers with peep-holes and walls with internal defences. From the keep, it is not only possible to see the green scenery and the grey valley of Teguise but also the coast of the island, the sea and even the shadowy profile of the nearby Fuerteventura. Nowadays , the castle has been fitted out to house the **Museo del Emigrante**, which recalls the role of emigrants from the Canaries in the development of America.

Santa Bárbara Castle

Famara

Famara beach, on the north of the island, extends along sevesal kilometres from the village of La Caleta, an old fishing centre, famous among gourmets for the quality of the fish to be had there. Battered constantly by the trade- winds coming from the Atlantic, the beach has a magnificent, wild look although it can be a little dangerous for bathers. Surfing enthusiasts on the other hand take full advantage of the waves and it is very much appreciated by those who go underwater fishing.

Famara Beach

La Caleta of Famara (creek)

Famara

Windmill

A panoramic view of Famara

Around the edge of the beach is a series of detached villas over looked by the amazing sheer walls of the Famara-Guatifay massif. From the highest peak on the island, the 670-metre Peñas del Cache, lovers of hang-gliding and delta-wing launch themselves into the air to glide over the cliffs to land to land on the beach. The Riscos de Famara, crags with the best botanical specimens on Lanzarote have a wide panorama of the islets that make up the Chinijo Archipelago.

Famara Beach

Haría

Aeolian Park

The Parque Eólico, with its modern wind-mills can be glimpsed on the right along the road between Teguise and Haría , before arriving at the **Mirador de Haría**. It is a good idea to stop here to take in the valley scenery with its oasis, its palm trees, its white houses and the spectacle that is the **Monte Corona volcano**. Almost 4000 years ago, the volcanic eruption caused an immense river of

A view of Haría

lava to cover the south-east and the north-east of the island. This formed the vast "*malpaís*" and the huge volcanic tube which includes the **Cueva de los Verdes** and the

Corona Mountain

Guinate Park

Jameos del Agua. There is an easy trail that leads up to the summit of Monte Corona, which looks down on the crater of the extinct volcano. This area is protected with the status of Monumento Natural.

Known also as "*Valle de las diez mil palmeras*" (Valley of the ten thousand palm trees), Haría is surprising for the greenness of its fertile fields breaking the arid volcanic tones of the island. Despite having been burned by Saracens in the not too distant past, it still has more palm trees than anywhere else on the island. Several local crafts are linked to the palm tree: basketry; work with "*pirganos*" (the dried petioles of the palm leaf), rattan and rosettes made from the fibres.

The people of Haría are emigrating to other parts of the island as tourism provides a more comfortable and more stable living than agriculture. The town is characterised by its dazzling white houses with their balconies and windows decorated with a grand profusion of flowers of all colours. The **Museo Sacro y Popular**, facing the peaceful main square of Haría, keeps old images and reiligious artefacts donated

A panoramic view of Haría

pregnant virgin, a controversial image by the Canario artist, Luján Pérez.

On the way to the **Mirador del Río** and next to the **Mirador de Guinate** you can visit the **Guinate Tropical Park**, specially equipped to keep around 1000 birds of different species from all over the world. The ever surprising antics of the parrots and cockatoos are always worth watching. A little further on, though isolated and difficult to find, is the **Bosquecillo**, the only forest on Lanzarote. The locals come here to spend Sunday afternoons and eat paella.

by the local people. Next to the museum, the Parish Church has a sculpture depicting a

Constitución Square

The Mirador del Río

In the extreme north of Lanzarote, the lofty Punta Fariones, a rocky spur of lava cuts into the sea like a knife. Between here and the the south eastern coast of the island of Graciosa of the Chinijo Archipelago is a stretch of sea known as *El Río*. At 479 metres, the Mirador del Río commands a fine view of the islets and the ocean, a seascape that will prove difficult to for-get. The Lanzaroteño artist César Manrique rebuilt what had been an old gun battery. He had a hollow cut into the mountain and built a restaurant inside. He put two domes in this huge space and then covered them with earth on which grass grew. In this way, thework remained hidden as if it formed part of the rock. The restaurant has a wide window, con-ceived by Manrique as a window on the cosmos, from which you can view in comfort a panora-ma of sea and sky so fantastic it seems unreal.

A view of Isla Graciosa from the Mirador del Río

Outside of the Mirador del Río

Mirador

A view of the Isla Graciosa

Outside and inside of the Mirador del Río

Archipiélago Chinijo

The Chinijo Archipelago ("chinijo" meaning "small" in the local vernacular) covers a total of 41 sq kilometres and was given the status of Natural Park in 1987 along with Risco de Famara to protect the landscape and its natural riches. It is comprised of the islands of La Graciosa, Alegranza and Montaña Clara and the islets of Roque del Este and Roque del Oeste or Roque del Infierno. The latter two are also nature reserves because of their interesting seabirds suchas shearwaters, ospreys, "grajos marinos", plovers, "tabobos", "guinchos", Eleonora's falcon and Berberia's falcon.

La Graciosa can be reached by boat from the **port of Órzola**. It is the biggest of the archipelago at 27 sq kilometres and the only one to be inhabited. Its permanent population of around 600 people is concentrated in a small town called **Caleta del Sebo** side by side with a fishing port. In fact, most of the inhabitants are involved with fishing as the surrounding waters are home to a fabulous reserve of fish among which species such as grouper, scorpion-fish, sole and John Dory abound.

Graciosa Isle (Caleta del Sebo and Las Conchas Beach)

Órzola, fishing tradition

Graciosa Island: Ferry

Los Jameos del Agua

Leaving the town of Órzola by the coast road you run through a region called **Malpaís de la Corona**, an area with Natural Monument status covered with the volcanic lava of eruptions that took place almost 4000 years ago. The contrast between the dark rocks and lava and the beaches and coves, some of which are the only ones on the island with fine white sand, makes this piece of coast very popular with bathers.

Malpaís of Corona

Inside of the Jameos del Agua

The field of petrified lava hides in its interior a chain of volcanic bubbles, caves and a long,wide tube that starts at the rim of the Mount Corona Volcano and submerges into the sea in what is known as the "Túnel del atlantico". This natural shaft, which is over 6 kilometres long, 15 metres high and the same width is the largest known lava tube in the world and is accessible from Jameos de Agua. "Jameo" is an indigenous word used to refer to a big cave, hollow or

Outside of the Jameos del Agua

Inside of the Jameos del Agua

Swimming-pool at the Jameos del Agua

volcanic bubble which has burst giving access from above.

The Jameos de Agua was the first architectural attraction designed by César Manrique, in 1968. From the entrance you go down 10 metres to reach the main gallery, 15 metres in diameter and 1625 metres long. Almost 70 metres below that is a huge lava cave with a lake below sea-level fed by small subterranean shafts. Some small, blind albino crabs which, from their appearance would seem to be better suited to the depths of the sea, live in it. This rare species is of great scientific interest and has become the symbol of the place. Further on is another volcanic bubble with a natural swimming pool and an exotic garden. Of all that has been installed, always in harmony with the environment, at Jameos de Agua perhaps the most outstanding is the **auditorium**. With seating for an audience of 600, a Festival of Visual Music is held here in October. It is also used for concerts, theatre and ballet. Likewise, the Casa de los Volcanes is a centre of volcanic phenomena both insular and global.

Gardens

Auditorium

Albino crab

Swimming-pool

Jameos del Agua

Cueva de los Verdes

One of the sections of the great lava tube created during the eruption of Monte Corona can be seen in the Cueva de los Verdes. It is made up of two galleries, one on top of the other. The one-hour guided tour follows corridors and laberynths, subterranean lakes and seemingly bottomless abysses, all expertly lit up to bring out the colours and shapes of the solidified lava. Inside the cave a human being seems very small indeed when compared to the immense power of nature. It is hard to imagine what the eruption that designed this great lava tube by chance must have been like. Thousands of Lanzaroteñoshave sought refuge in its bowels in days gone by to save their lives when pirate raids razed the island. One of the more spacious galleries houses an auditorium that holds 1000 people and various musical performances are occasionally put on.

Entrance to the Cueva

Inside of the Cueva de los Verdes

La Garita Beach

Jardín de Cactus

Heading south from Jameos del Agua and the Cueva de los Verdes you arrive at **Arrieta** and la playa de la Garita, a beach shielded from the wind as are those of Caleta del Campo and Punta Mujeres. It is an area where fish and other species such as the limpet, so prized by the canarios abound. The landscape between Arrieta and Mala is unusual: "tuneras" (pricky pear trees), "piteras" and "tabaibas" adorn the barren earth and crags. Between Mala and **Guatiza** lie enormous cactus fields used for the breeding of cochineal, a small insect imported from Mexico, whose larvae produce a red dye much valued for its

Lake at the garden

Prickly pears with woodlouse

A partial view of the Cactus Garden

Guatiza windmill and cactus

A variety of cactus

quality and fastness before the discovery of aniline.

Around this agricultural landscape and at the foot of the Guatiza mill, the multi-faceted artist, César Manrique conceived the Jardín de Cactus, a study centre for the flora of the area. In the shape of a Roman circus, along the stone paths and between the black ash are over 1,400 species and almost 10,000 plants. Most of the cacti comes from America, although there are some from Madagascar and the Canary Islands as well. Some grow to only 2 or 3 centimetres, while others can reach a height of 25 metres, each species a different shape.

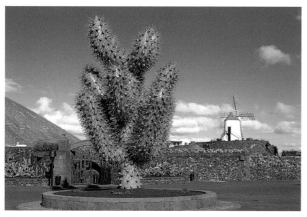

Entrance to the Cactus Garden

Ways of stones and black ashes

San Bartolomé

The town that the indigenous population of Lanzarote called *Ajei* has always been linked to the evolution and history of the **jable**, a word derived from the French *sable* (sand), "jable" is one of the indigenous ways of cultivating the earth used by the

An old windmill

House Ajei

Tanit Museum

islanders, who have converted dry land into fertile soil. Along the so-called "corridor of jable", between the western half of Teguise and the north of San Bartolomé, the sand from the beach at Famara is in constant motion, blown by the trade-winds and on its way, covering the groung until arriving at **Playa Honda** and the tourist coast at Tías. These whitish limestone sands of organic origin contain nutrients which are very good for certain plants such as the red sweet potatoe, melons, water-melons, potatoes and other vegetables. The farmers protect their crops from the Saharan Siroccos by putting up huge barriers; fences made of straw and cereal stalks fixed into the earth.

In the 18th century, Francisco Guerra Clavijo y Perdomo, Governor and Chief of the militia on Lanzarote settled in San Bartolomé. Guerra and his descendants became the owners of nearly all the municipality. In 1787, Cayetano Guerra ordered the building of the church of San Bartolomé, which in 1796 became the **parish church**, and in which romanic carvings such as the one of San Amaro are kept. Among the civic buildings which stand out in this quiet town are the **house/palace of Mayor Guerra,** the

Playa Honda and Commercial Centre

Tanit Museum and, especially, the **Casa Ajei**, a señorial construction with cottages behind it for the tenant farmers who worked in the fields.

The town of San Bartolomé is surrounded by **archaeological sites** of the first order. An example is **Zonzamas**, the most important remains of the ancient people of the Canaries. The last chief of the *Majos* , Guargafrá lived here among the "casas hondas", one of the kinds of primitive dwellings on the island. Of most historic and scientific interest are the so-called "queseras de Zonzamas" which owe their name to their similarity to enormous containers for making cheese. They were built on flat surfaces on basalt and had parallel channels several metres long and grooves inside.

House-Palace of the Mayor Guerra

The Town Hall Square

Museo al Campesino (Peasant Museum)

The connection between this area and the cultivation of the soil gave César Manrique the idea for the "Museo al Campesino" as a homage to the work of the men and women in the fields. The 15 metres high sculpture, "Monument to Fertility" is dedicated to the forgotten efforts of the unknown peasant of Lanzarote. Between San Bartolomé and **Mozaga**, in the middle of the island, the monument was designed by Manrique and made by Jesús Coto in 1968. Coto used old water tanks from fishing boats and yachts that he welded and painted white to represent the peasant and his livestock. Close to the sculpture is the **Museo al Campesino**, a restored and enlarged cottage, in which César Manrique wanted to see the old island way of life reflected faithfully. The Museum shows domestic utensils and tools used by the island´s farmers, throughout history, to work, to plough, to harvest, to carry and to store the fruits of the earth. You can try traditional Canaries cooking, based on the products and culinary traditions of Lanzarote in the restaurant.

Monument to Fecundity

Traditional loom

Popular crafts

"Sancocho"; a Canary meal

A panoramic view of the Museo del Campesino

Traditional cooking

Handmade products

Monument to Fecundity

Museum del Campesino (Peasant Museum)

Typical restaurant

Tías

The town of Tías rises on a small gently sloping ridge, within a municipality situated in the Paisaje Pretegido (Protected Landscape) of La Gería and looking down towards the most important tourist coast of the island. Tías owes its origins to the fact that the two big fortunes of the island were inherited by the daughters Francisca and Hernanda Fajardo, who were related to Alfonso Fajardo, Governor of Gran Canaria. They were both spinsters and left their property to their nephews, which is why the municipality has ever since been called *Tías de Fajardo* (Fajardos´s Aunts). This town retains still today the tradition of La Santa (Saint Lucia): the young men and women take advantage of the vigil to the saint for their courting. The locality is also famous for its music groups that maintain the roots of a particular musical harvest. Tías has a Municipal Theatre and a Museo de Arte Grabado. The parish is dedicated to the Virgen de la Candelaria, whose church built in 1796, was restored in 1872 after several fires.

Fariones Hotel: the beach

Puerto del Carmen

20 kilometres of low flat coastline extend southwards from Arrecife with the best natural beaches anywhere on the island. The most important tourist resort is Puerto del Carmen, a short distance from Lanzarote airport. Hotels and apartments have been built here in recent years but always respecting traditional architec-

Matagorda

Puerto Calero

Matagorda Beach

ture with low-rise whitewashed buildings. 64% of the island´s tourist accommodation is, here, but even so, care has been taken to integrate the buildings and facilities with the environment. The same is true of nearby **Puerto Calero**. Puerto del Carmen was originally a sea port, an atmosphere that still prevails in the small fishing port in the old quarter known as La Tiosa, still used by fishing boats and pleasure boats.

Los Pocillos

The usual catch in this area consists of sardines, "bogas", "salemas", "viejas" and tuna, which are prepared for sale in the port itself. The daily routine of the seaman and their work on land attracts the attention of visitors on the Varadero esplanade.

Puerto del Carmen has 6 kilometres of golden sands. **Playa Grande**, in the middle, is the most popular; *Pocillos* is the biggest but also the quietest; *Matagorda* is good for windsurfing, and *Guacimetá*, is secluded and surrounds part of the runway of the Airport. There are also little coves between volcanic ledges such as *Pila de la Barrilla, La Chica, La Peóita and Barranquillo*. Little cruises along the coast or day-trips to Fuerteventura, Lobo or the beaches at Papagayo in the south of Lanzarote can be taken from the quay. It is also possible to hire boats for deep-sea fishing at several miles from the coast.

Playa Grande

Playa Grande

Playa Grande

The dry dock (varadero) of Puerto del Carmen

Playa Grande

Los Pocillos

Playa Grande

Los Pocillos

Avenue of Las Playas

Playa Chica

Pier of the Playa Chica

Dry dock (varadero)

Maritime avenue of Playa Grande

Matagorda

Dry dock (varadero) of Puerto del Carmen

Typical restaurants at the dry dock (varadero)

The visitor can choose between more than 250 restaurants in Puerto del Carmen, especially in *La Tiñosa*, where they offer specialities of fresh fish prepared in the traditional way served with the traditional "papas arrugadas", "mojo" and "gofio". There are also plenty of shops and bazaars to buy crafts, clothes or electric appliances along the Avenida de las Playas. The same can be said about entertainment as there is ample and varied nightlife centred around Centro Comercial Atlántico, mainly for young people, although there are other places such as the Casino, quiet open air bars, live music and night clubs.

The 'fiestas' en Puerto del Carmen are one of its principal attactions. The main one takes place in the last week of July and the first week of August in honour of the Virgen del Carmen when there is a procession of boats. There are also lively fairs and dances on the magical night of San Juan and, especially, during **Carnival**. Although every municipality on Lanzarote has Carnival, and the Arrecife might claim the biggest crowds, Carnival in Puerto del Carmen is one of the most spectacular with its big parade, of several kilometres along Avenida de las Playas, celebrated the first Saturday after Ash Wednesday.

Commercial Centre

Fresh fish

Church of the Virgen del Carmen

La Geria

Between Mozaga and Yaiza, in the middle of the island, is one of the most unusual landscapes on Lanzarote, La Geria. The volcanic eruptions of Timanfaya in the 18th century covered the most fertile land on the island bringing ruin to the islanders. However, the peasants turned what appeared to be disaster into an ingenious resource, using the lava to farm through curious and original means. In La Geria, fig trees, vines and other fruit trees are planted in the hollows that the lava flows left or in trenches, sometimes several metres deep, dug into the volcanic ash,

Collecting grapes

La Geria

A panoramic view of La Geria

Wine barrels and Timanfaya at the back

giving access to the soil below. To protect the crops from the wind, little semi-circular walls called "zocos" are used. When they saw what good results these natural sandings had, they built their artificial ones so they covered the fields with soil over which they spread a layer of *lapilli* (fragments of volcanic rock) or volcanic ash, known on the island as "picón" or "rofe". During the night, the "rofe" allowed the humidity through to the vegetal soil and during the day prevented its evaporation. Thanks to this technique, melons, water-melons, tomatoes, potatoes, onions, garlic and corn have been grown without irrigation. However, the crop which attracts the most attention is the vast extension of vines with their green leaves resting on the black ash and each one protected in its hole from whose grapes comes the legendary **Malvasía wine**. This is a fresh, strong golden wine marking the victory of the tenacity of the lanzaroteño peasant over the hostile earth. The road that runs along the valley of La Geria has become one of the most frequented tourist routes. Visitors make stops in various bodegas such as '*El Grifo*', where there is also a '*Museo del Vino*' or '*La Geria*', to see the manufacturing process and to taste and buy the results.

Museum of Wine

A panoramic view of La Geria

A partial view of La Geria

Uga

The town of Uga, in La Geria, is similar to those of north Africa due to its white houses in the form of a cube. It is built over the primitive village of the same name, buried under a 10 metre thick layer by the volcanic eruption of Timanfaya. One of Canary-style wrestling´s most legendary representatives, The *Pollo de Uga*, now deceased, made Uga famous as he was born there. To reach Uga, it is necessary to cross the north part of the valley of **Femés**, the oldest village on Lanzarote. It was in this historic town,

Church of San Marcial del Rubicón

Uga

wrapped in silence and dazzling white that a church in honour of San Marcial was built. An 18th century carving of San Marcial de Rubicón, the patron saint of Lanzarote, is kept there among arches and very decorated poles. In the festival of San Marcial, held in Femés during the the first week of July, the famous "coplas" and "endechas canarias" are performed. **Los Ajaches**, atop its ancient massif can be found a few kilometres away. It is protected with the category of Monumento Natural with important endemic volcanic species and has the second highest peak on the island, the Atalaya de Femés (608 metres).

Playa Blanca

In the far south of Lanzarote there is an old fishing centre which keeps some of the marine flavour that characterise its past, Playa Blanca. This is despite having been turned into one of the best tourist resorts on the island. Modern hotels and luxury developments, always white, have been built in this quiet and privileged environment of golden sands, and calm, clear, blue waters. Fuerteventura can be reached from its little port in just over half an hour on the daily

Los Ajaches seen from the Mirador of Femés

Maritime avenue and beach

Rubicón

ferry. Close to Playa Blanca, the **Papagayo** ledge at the foot of Los Ajaches Massif, is surrounded by excellent beaches and secluded coves which are practically untouched. It seems as though time has stood still in this astonishing place, as if nothing is important except drinking in the scenery, swimming, diving, sunbathing and, above all, relaxing and resting.

This part of the island is called El Rubicón and it is where the French colonisers and adventurers Jean de Bethencourt and Gadifer de Lasalle settled at the beginning of the 15th century. On one of the beaches of Papagayo a castle, the **Castillo de las Coloradas**, was built. Also known as "Torre de Águila" (Eagle Tower), it was constructed in 1742 to keep watch over the Straits of La Bocayna, the 15-kilometre arm of the sea

Castle of Las Coloradas

Papagayo Beach

Playa Dorada

Rubicón

Playa Blanca

separating Lanzarote and Fuerteventura. The small fortress, which belongs to Patrimonio Histórico Nacional, has two circular storeys and an "isabelino" style bell-tower. It was burnt and destroyed by pirates loking for slaves and livestock during the reign of Carlos III. A magnificent panorama of the coast of Fuerteventura and the islet of Lobos can be admired from its terraces.

A night view of Playa Blanca

Pedestrian street

Ferry to Fuerteventura

Papagayo Beach

Papagayo

Flamingo Beach

Salinas de Janubio (Janubio saltworks)

Fishing has always been important on Lanzarote and this has given rise to other industries such as salt production, to supply the boats fishing off the coasts of Africa. To this end the natural lagoons that formed on the coast were turned into saltworks. The natural lagoon of Janubia, in the municipality of Yaiza, was the most important of all. The majority of the salt needed by the island fishing industry was produced here in hundreds of mud and earth containers, which looked like a huge chessboard. The windmills used to draw the sea- water up to them are still standing. During the evaporation process, the water changes colour from an intense blue to the blinding white of the heaps of salt, which are in stark contrast to the dark lava of the nearby terrain. Victor Fernández , 'El Salinero' , who died in Yaiza in 1920 at 76 years of age, created the complicated structures at Janubio. He also composed a fine collection of 'coplas canarias' (traditional songs) that are performed in holiday and celebrations even today. Near the saltworks is Janubio beach flanked by the Punta del Volcán.

Saltworks of Janubio

Los Hervideros

Los hervideros is a fragment of steeply sloping coast between Salinas de Janubio and El Golfo that like so many places on Lanzarote demonstrate the ever surprising spectacle of nature. The cooling and solidification of lava formed subterranean tubes, deep crevices and galleries or shafts. A constant battering of the waves forces water up hidden nooks and it suddenly spurts out of the surface like a pressure cooker, roaring and creating great mountains of white foam.

Los Hervideros

El Golfo

Near Los Hervideros skirting Montaña Bermeja is El Golfo. Of volcanic origin, it is a crater formed during the eruptions of the 18th century and eroded by the sea to the shape of a Roman amphitheatre. A lovely lagoon, between 8 and 10 metres deep, has been created by the filtration of sea-water into the bottom of what is left of the cone. Its intense emerald green colour stands out against the black lava and the clear blue of the ocean. The 'Lanzaroteños' call this place Laguna Verde (Green Lagoon) or **Charco Los Clicos** and the strange 'olivinas', semi-precious stones with which local craftsmen create original jewellery are found here. Nearby, is a small town famous all over the island for the exquisite fresh fish that can be tried there.

Montaña Bermeja

Charco de los Clicos or Laguna Verde

Looking for olivines

Olivine

Charco de Los Clicos

El Golfo (the Gulf) at dusk

Church of Nuestra Señora de los Remedios

Yaiza

Yaiza is a name of Guanche origin and the town was founded by peasants who had emigrated from the Iberian Peninsula during the first period of colonisation. Now, it is one of the biggest and most attractive municipalities, from a tourist point of view, on Lanzarote. The Parque Nacional of

Windmill

Typical house

A panoramic view of Yaiza

Rural hotel

Timanfaya, La Geria, Los Ajaches, the beaches of Papagayo, Las Salinas de Janubio, Los Hervideros and El Golfo as well as the towns of Femés, Las Breñas, Playa Blanca and Yaiza itself all belong to it . Despite its proximity to Timanfaya, the town escaped the sea of lava during the eruptions and it is one of the best towns of the archipelago, with its simple architecture, its whitness and its well-maintained streets adorned with a great variety of flowers and plants. The church of Nuestra Señora de los Remedios in Yaiza has several interesting carvings of that Virgin.

A typical restaurant: "La Era"

The Timanfaya National Park seen from Yaiza

Timanfaya

Between 1730 and 1736 west-central Lanzarote shook and the bowels of the earth cracked. For six years explosions, tremors and lava flows did not cease. The smoke and gases poisoned the goat herds and at least 23 hamlets were buried. The centre of volcanic activity was in the Macizo del Fuego or de Timanfaya, where more than 25 craters covered 20,000 hectares with lava, ashes, volcanic bombs and rock transforming the fertile plains into a desolate, blackeneded and hostile landscape. Although there were no human victims of these violent eruptions, under these mountains, slopes and deserts of

Timanfaya National Park

Timanfaya

Volcanic lava

petrified lava called '*malpaís*', the villages of Tingafa, Mancha Blanca, Maretes, Santa Carolina, San Juan, Masdache, Peña Palomas, Timanfaya,Testeina, La Geria and Los Rodeos will lie buried forever.

'On the first day of September 1730, between 9 and 10 o'clock at night, the earth suddenly opened up. Close to Timanfaya, a gigantic mountain rose up spitting enormous flames that burned incessantly for 19 days,' is how Yaiza parish priest Andrés Lorenzo recorded events for posterity. Other passages in his account explain that: 'At times, the lava ran like water, while at others it was calm like a trickle of honey.' The darkness, ashes and smoke

Lava sea and route of camels

Timanfaya

drove away the people of Yaiza and environs on more than one occasion. The end of the six years of intense volcanic activity led to a period of peace and quiet. This was shattered when in 1824, another eruption lasting from July 31st to October 25th opened up three new mouths in Tao, Tinguatón and Nuevo although it had much less impact than that of the previous century.

Montaña Ortiz

The National Park

Situated between the municipalities of Yaiza and Tinajo the Parque Nacional de Timanfaya, the maximun protection for a natural space, was created in 1974 in those areas where volcanic activity had been most intense and it covers a surface area of 542 sq kilomertres. It is an inorganic mineral world, a desolate landscape, unique and surprising, covered with lava and ash. The craters of **Montaña del Fuego**, Caldera Rajada, Montaña Encantada and Monte Rajada emerge dark, red, brown and gold. At the

The National Park at dusk

Montaña del Fuego

Caldera de Corazoncillo

Montaña Testeyna

Caldera Rajada and Quemada and Encantada Mountains

Lying down camels

Lying down camels

the park that register some geothermic activity, which the specialists call 'anomaly'. The best known are those that are shown to tourists on the **Islote de Hilario**, where the temperature reaches 400°C at a depth of 2 metres. In a little excavation,

entrance to the National Park, signposted with the embliem of an imp, the idea of 'Lanzaroteño' artist, César Manrique, is the Museo de Rocas. Here you can get information about the routes you can follow during the visit. The shortest is around 20 minutes and starts in the **Echadero de Camellos**, for those interested in trying this exotic means of transport to follow the well-marked paths of the Montañas del Fuego.

Although Timanfaya is a 'cold' area, there are some 7,000 sq metres within

Diablillo (little devil)

Timanfaya

Route of camels

A camel in the Timanfaya National Park

A volcano alignment

Sunset at the Timanfaya National Park

we can see how the '*Majorera*' gorse catches fire in a moment, while if water is poured into a little hole in the ground it evaporates immediatly in an unbelievable way and with a deafening noise, the geyser phenomenon. In this place, so-called because a man named Hilario lived here with the sole company of his camel, César Manrique

Geothermic show

Geothermic show

designed the **Restaurante El Diablo** (The Devil), a circular building with a façade covered in volcanic stone perfectly integrated into its environment. Inside, visitors can see a well some 5 metres deep, with a temperature of between 80 and 200ºC, heat that rises from the bowels of the earth and is used as a natural oven by the restaurant kitchen.

El Diablo Restaurant

El Diablo Restaurant: the oven

Ruta de los Volcanes (Route of the volcanoes)

An invisible path, perfectly camouflaged in its environment, goes some 14 kilometres into the National Park: the route of the volcanoes, which starts and finishes on the Islet of Hilario. Doing the route on foot or in private cars is not allowed.

Timanfaya is a very fragile natural space, a simple footstep can take decades to disappear. A Lanzarote council bus does the journey in around 50 minutes and explanations of what can be seen are given in several languages and various

Route of the Volcanoes

stops are made at some of the more amazing places en route. The **Mirador de Montaña Rajada** is one such place and from here the best part of the Park and the coast can be seen or you can simply marvel at the fanciful shapes of the blocks of petrified lava in close up. The route goes through volcanic tunnel, passes next to several 'hornitos' and enables you to admire the bottom of some craters.

Montaña Rajada

Hornito (small oven)

A bus route through the Park

Valle de la Tranquilidad (Tranquillity Valley)

Cráter of Timanfaya

Volcanic lava

Valle de la Tranquilidad (Tranquillity Valley)

El Pajarito Volcano

Los Azulejos

Landscape in the Park

A lava sea

Route of the Volcanoes

Route of the Volcanoes

103

blanco' a small shrub with gnarled branches and leaves that are almost white. 'Tabaibas', 'berodes', hawthorn, thyme, and rushes among other species are examples of this unexpected plant presence that persists in living in this amazing landscape. Between the cavities in the volcanic rocks Haría lizards are often seen scurrying here and there or sunning themselves. They mea-

One of the most surprising things in this place where nature is apparently dead is the existence of plant life amid the lava and ashes. Up to 180 species of lichen coat the hard volcanic rock and colour them in shades of light grey or yelow. There are also plants that can only be found on the island of Lanzarote such as the 'tojío' with its bright yellow flowers, 'la lengua de vaca' with blue flowers and the 'salado

Lichens and vegetation at the Timanfaya National Park

sure only 20 centimetres and have adapted perfectly to the harsh conditions of the area. Blackish or grey they feed on insects and the scarce vegetable matter that they come across. Another reptile, the 'peringuén majorero' is also very well adapted to this environment. The 'musaraña' (shrew) is the only endemic mammal of the islands. The 'paloma brava', a kind of dove, makes its nest among the solidified lava while various bird species: crows, Egyptian vultures, shearwaters, gulls, geese, gannets, ducks and egrets fly in the ever blue skies of the National Park.

The only journey you can make on foot in Timanfaya is to Tremasana although it is necessary to go with a park guide. On the other hand, the coast line between Piedra de Ventura and Playa del Paso has free access. The excursion means a four or five hour trek through the blocks of magma that stopped at the sea.

Walking trip

Interpretation Centre

Valle de la Tranquilidad (Tranquillity Valley)

A trip by jeep

Tinajo

Despite its outwardly arid appearance, Tinajo is the larder of Lanzarote thanks to the richness and quality of its soil and its orientation to the trade winds. Within its municipal borders all the peculiar agricultural methods of Lanzarote are used: sand both natural and artificial, jable and the almost exotic agricultural technique, 'gavias'. These are parcels of land with deep, fertile soil on the slopes of ravines surrounded by compacted earth walls watered by them flooding with the rain water that runs down the ravine.The

Caldera del Cuchillo and Sóo

Tiagua

importance of agriculture to the area is reflected in the interesting **Museo Agrícola**, which can be visited in the hamlet of **Tiagua** to the south east of Tinajo. The Museum, also known as "El Patio" is on a great restored estate which in its day was a model farm as much for the variety of its production as its well-designed rustic and colonial architecture.

In the eastern part of the municipality close to the village of Sóo is the great '**Caldera del cuchillo**', whose southern cliff is bow-shaped. The most westerly part is partially included in the Timanfaya National Park where it is possible to visit the spectacular volcanic cone of Caldera Blanca.

Tinajo is characterised by the onion-shaped chimneys that crown many of its white houses, a clear example of the popular architecture of Lanzarote. In its parish church of San Roque, with its huge naves and 'mudejar' ceiling, is a

Agricultural Museum

Christ attributed to Luján Pérez and a precious carving of the Virgen de la Candelaria by the sculptor Fernando Estévez. However, the most venerated Virgin in Tinajo is the Virgen de los Dolores, known hereabouts as the Virgin of the Volcanoes, who symbolises the redemption of the island´s suffering. A legend tells of how this Virgin was carried before the lava that threatened the village during the 18th century eruption of Montaña Colorada and she was able to stop the flow.The **Ermita de los Dolores**, built in Mancha Blanca in 1736 and across symbolises this divine intervention.Something similar happened in the eruption of 1824 of the Clérigo Huarte volcano.

Nuestra Señora de los Volcanes

Hermitage of los Dolores

La costa de La Santa

The municipality of Tinajo faces the sea along a wide stretch of coast between La Boca de Abajo and Peña Dorada whose north-east sector has been urbanised in the service of tourism. Next to the old maritime village of La Santa, the sports-tourist complex **Club La Santa** is notable for its magnificent natural swimming pools, which are connected to the sea. The sports facilities at the Club are the best of the whole island and elite athletes from America and Europe, especially the Nordic countries come here to train and rest. It is no surprise given the fine

La Santa

La Santa Club

La Santa Club

facilities and quiet relaxed atmosphere that the professionals of football, basketball and athletics choose here for the pre-season and winter get-togethers. It also offers excellent conditions for windsurfing.

Every year, in the last week of May, the Club La Santa organises the toughest test of the triathlon (cycling, swimming and marathon running) '**Ironman**', which is only held in nine places on the planet. Over 500 athletes from all over the world compete in this spectacular trial which takes place on different parts of the island and it is quite an event for 'Lanzaroteños' and visitors alike.

Opposite this development, in the middle of the bay, is the natural phenomenon of **La Isleta**. It is a reef barely above the surface of the sea. As it is not very deep this submarine platform offers excellent possibilities for fishing both from the surface and under water. In the environs of the coast of La Santa is the famous **cave of Ana Viciosa**, which features in several old legends. Around 1650, the legendary Viciosa, Señora of Montaña Clara and wife of the Governor, Juan de León Moxica, owned practically the whole area. It is said that the promiscuous lady had amorous adventures in the cave with young peasants who she later thanked by freeing them or presenting them with a plot of her land.

La Isleta

La Santa Club

Índex